ETERNAL
RISING

Inspiring Your Greater Potential and Illuminating Your Way

JOHNNY BLACKBURN

Copyright © 2019 Johnny Blackburn

All rights reserved. No part of this publication may be reproduced, distributed, or transmitted in any form or by any means, including photocopying, recording, or other electronic or mechanical methods, without the prior written permission of the publisher, except for brief quotations embodied in critical reviews and certain other noncommercial uses permitted by copyright law.

Printed in the United States of America by Ingram Spark Publishing.

First Printing, 2019
Second Revision Edition, 2022
Third Revision Edition, 2025

ISBN 0692941754

Cover Image: Shutterstock
Editor: Melanie Buntin

Presence Academy, Inc.
San Diego, California
www.johnnyblackburn.net

Dedication

May this work
be an honoring
to this great evolutionary process
living through us all—
the Eternal Rising.

This book was written through inspiration,
by the authors own hand and
no artificial intelligence was used in its writing.

As humanity continues to evolve through the Digital Age
it appears that AI, robotics and automation
will be increasingly integrated into modern living.

May we use these tools to enrich
some areas of our lives, while continuing
to cultivate our own intelligence, creativity and virtue.

And may we continue to grow our own
abilities and activate our greater potential,
while leveraging the enhancements of technology
as we continue to evolve in co-creating
a better, brighter world for us all.

The Eternal Rising of the Phoenix

The mythic story of the phoenix is a powerful tale of resilience, renewal, emergent evolution, and the cyclical nature of time.

According to the legend, the great phoenix is said to be drawn to fly toward the Sun—a symbol of the Source of Life. And though one individual will not make it in its own lifetime, the phoenix can't not fly upward toward the Source. Yet, out of its ashes a new phoenix arises, reborn from the remains of its predecessor.

The next phoenix is said to be just as beautiful and powerful as the one that came before—representing the power to overcome adversity and emerge even stronger in subsequent evolutions.

Thus, the phoenix's transformation can be seen as a metaphor for personal and spiritual evolution—a timeless reminder of the cyclical nature of life, the power of renewal, the collective contribution to evolution and the enduring spirit on its journey back to the Source.

Just like some of you, who might not see the fruits of your labors and the impact of your contribution fully manifest in the world in your own lifetime. Yet, inspired by something greater, you and we continue flying upwards—repeatedly dying and being reborn, carrying and passing the torch—illuminating and actualizing individual and collective potential, unfolding over vast timescapes that exceed the limits of a single being or life.

And in this way, your personal growth, the betterment of your life and those around you, is an inseparable part of the whole—linked by the interconnectedness of Life and lifetimes. We are all part of something greater and together we are contributing to the collective evolution of consciousness—the Eternal Rising.

*"The evolution of the world
depends on the evolution
of the individual."*

| Sri Aurobindo |

Table of Contents

Dedication	v
The Eternal Rising of the Phoenix	ix
Table of Contents	xi
Eternal Rising	xv

Living Deeply

Glory Rising	2
Waking Beauty	3
I Still See the Spark	4
Echoes of Time	5
The Standard of Your Soul	6
Choosing to be Here	7
Fear as Your Teacher	9
Tired Truths	11
Your Vehicle for the Experience	12
Soul Check	13
Mystery Unfolding	14
At the End of Your Days	16
Freedom in the Face of Death	17
The Ultimate Embrace	21
Your Time is Limited	22
The True Privilege	23
True Legacy	24
Living Deeply	25

Growth

Growing Bright	28
I Hope You Make the Best of It	29
Slowly Though Forward	30
Remember When Waking	31
The Pain of Waste	32
Expanding or Clinging	33
Growing or Going Through It	34
Ready to Grow	35

Lifeforces	36
Easier and Better	37
On Growing and Becoming	38
What is the Lesson?	39
The Paradox of Change	40
Adulting	41
To the Wonder	42
Personal Growth and Beyond	43
It's Been Her this Whole Time	44

HEALING

The Way Beyond is Through	48
Your Body Keeps Score	49
Wisdom in the Sensations	50
For When You are Ready	51
Your Pain and Potential	52
Little "T" Trauma	53
The Varieties of Wound Experiences	54
Why is This Coming Up Now?	56
Language of the Body	57
Reassigning Protectors	58
Grieve Fully	60
Soul Knowing	62
Heart Pull	63
At Peace With the Past	64
The Source at the Center	65

PURPOSE

Why are You Here?	68
What's Yours to Do?	69
How to Live With Purpose	70
Living Your Purpose	71
This Instinct Inside You	73
Inspiration Not Insignificance	74
Deep Dedication	76
Aim High	77
Life Beckons you	78
Purpose Prayer	79

Virtue

Soul Uploads	82
Character Emanation	83
Respect	84
Grit	85
Less of This, More of That	86
Embodiment	87
Skillfulness	88
Precision	89
Sovereignty	90
Discernment	92
Higher Guidance	94
Wisdom Wanting to Speak Through You	95
Intentional Flow	96
Manifesting	97
Joyful Contagion	98
Embodied Presence	99
The Ascendant Bow	100
Wise and Loving	101
The Giving of Your Greatness	102

Evolution

Whispers From the Future	106
The Evolution of Life on Planet Earth	107
Ashes to Ashes, Stardust to Dust	109
The Evolutionary Impulse	111
The Great Chain	112
Come Together	113
Seven Generations	114
Humanity in the Age of Technology	115
What Will You Do Then?	116
Evolutionary Cultivation	117
Span of Awareness	118
Receiver of the Future	119

Wayshowers

Explorers of Experience	122
Ripples of Betterment	123

Keep Going Towards the Light 124
Luminaries 125
Glory Smiling Through 126
Ambassadors of Love 127
Pointing Others to the Light 128
Path Carvers 129
Mystics of the Ages 130
It's Safe This Time 131
Stay Bright and Upright 133
Leadership in Times Like Now 134
Evolutionary Emissaries 135
That Which Lives Through You 136
Living Legacy 137
To the Mystics and the Wayshowers 138

GRATITUDE AND ACKNOWLEDGMENTS 140

ABOUT THE AUTHOR: MY RISING 141

Eternal Rising

What is this drive inside the Phoenix
that compels it, ceaselessly, toward the Sun,
rising again and again from its own ashes,
even if it won't reach it in its own lifetime?

And in this world
there are also
extraordinary humans
inspired by something
greater than themselves
who continue to rise,
sometimes amidst difficult
or challenging circumstances,
or while facing peril and persecution.

And through the
contribution of their lives,
become part of a great
evolutionary process
of bettering, brightening
and beautifying our world.

They are the mission-driven businesses,
working to create a better world,
the loving parents who are healing themselves,
and giving their children better opportunities,
the artists who continue create and beautify,
even if their work isn't publicly recognized,
the inventors who still innovate
even if they are scorned, threatened
or have their work destroyed,
the spiritual mystics dedicated to Awakening,
despite persecution, torture and death,
and the change agents across cultures,
passionately working for social justice and equality.

We salute those courageous
and committed beings
who forged the pathways
of greater human potential
who have devoted their lives
to the love, liberation
and evolution of life on Planet Earth.

We've gone further
by standing on the shoulders of giants,
like the great mythic phoenix
who continues to fly towards the sun,
driven by something greater
than just its own personal concerns
and though it perishes in the process,
out of its ashes rises another
and the contribution expressed
through the life over time
empowering the collective
to evolve again and again,
eternally rising,
all rising up.

PART 1

LIVING
DEEPLY

Glory Rising

Looking back at the end,
you'll feel the glory,
in the character you cultivated,
the contribution you created
and the ripple of the wake
of the way you walked
through this world.

The honor, the dignity
and the true triumph lives,
not in never failing,
but in how you
continued rising
after the times you fell.

WAKING BEAUTY

Everything has beauty,
but you have to feel it in your heart,
to see it through your eyes.

I Still See the Spark

I appreciate your humanness,
the way you laugh,
the vulnerability of your heart,
your endearing quirks.

I see the pain in your eyes too,
but underneath all of that,
I see a spark in you,
sensing there's something more,
a glimmer of the Eternal.

Learn to appreciate your own humanity and the humanity in others.

Echoes of Time

I see you
as you have been,
in the embodiment
of the past
that's shaped your present
and the character
etched into your being
by your lived experience.

I see you
as you are now,
in the depth of your being
and the expanse of Presence.

I see you
as you can be,
in the glimmers from the future,
beckoning you forward
toward your greater potential,
whispering to be lived through you.

The Standard of Your Soul

Your life may be
uncomfortable or painful
when you are living below
the standard of your Soul.

That's one of the ways
Life inspires you to grow.

So then maybe
this is your opportunity,
your calling,
to rise up
to what your Soul knows
is the reach of your potential.

Choosing to be Here

Have you
fully chosen to be here?

And when I say 'you'
I mean your Soul,
your deeper essence,
that which takes 'your' life,
underneath the masks and persona,
beyond birth, aging and death.

And when I say 'here'
I mean on Planet Earth
in the Milky Way Galaxy
amidst this vast Universe.

So, have you
fully chosen to be here,
for the duration of the experience,
fully inhabiting your body,
deeply engaged in your life,
making the best of
what you were given,
learning, growing,
enjoying and loving?

If not,
is there a part of you that is scared
of being in your body,
feeling emotion,
connecting with others
or the physical world?

If not,
do you feel like you don't belong?
Or do you have regrets
about how you've been living?

Well, I hope you are
able to feel and release,
whatever is in the way
of you fully choosing your life.

Remember why you're here.
Choose to do what you came to do.
You don't have to,
which is part of the
power of the choice.
Though you may want to
before your body's last breath,
so you don't have to learn
the same lessons again next time.

Fear as Your Teacher

Observe your fears,
trace them all the way down,
find their roots in your body,
fully feel it, until it releases.

If after fully accepting and feeling it
it hasn't released
ask the fear what it's about.

Maybe it is pointing you to limiting beliefs,
protecting you to keep you safe,
guiding you to enhance your life,
or maybe you need to face that fear to grow.

Did you ever think
fear could be your teacher?

These are some major soul lessons,
we have the opportunity to master
in this human experience:
Fear of Germs & Sickness.
Fear of Connection.
Fear of Loss.
Fear of Life.
Fear of Death.

Some may be easy for you,
others may really challenge you.
But when your fears go unacknowledged
or stay below conscious awareness
they can keep you stuck,
have you avoid important areas of life,
limit your freedom,
overwhelm you,
or get projected out

onto all kinds of bogeys and threats,
which may not even really exist.

Face your fears.
The way out is through them.
Learn to embrace them
feeling and listening, before releasing.
They may be teaching you about life.
or they may be the gatekeepers
to your true freedom,
greater empowerment,
enjoyment of the journey,
while trusting Life's guidance.

What are you afraid of?

Tired Truths

If you get tired,
try resting
instead of quitting.

If you get tired,
you might need to
take better care of your health.

If you get tired,
maybe you can manage
your energy better,
so you don't burn out.

Or maybe,
if you get tired,
it's simply time
to do something else.

What has made you weary?

Your Vehicle for the Experience

Your energetic and nervous systems
together serve as
receivers and transmitters of experience,
with immense latent potential,
limited only by your beliefs,
undeveloped capacities and
the openness of your channels.

Release past body-stored trauma,
clear limiting beliefs.
learn to deeply relax,
find safety in your body
and live with an open heart.
Be grounded in your feet and legs,
fully choose to be here,
take ownership of your body
and responsibility for your life.

Then, open its energetic channels,
creating the space and potency
to activate your greater potential,
so you can joyfully thrive,
contribute your purpose,
give and receive love,
and Awaken as the One Awareness.

If you knew it was your vehicle for experience, would you take better care of it and activate its potential?

Soul Check

How does your Higher Self feel
about the way you are using
the first hour of each day
to activate your system
opening, aligning
and powering up for the day
while actualizing
your greater potential over time?

Is there anything else it
would like to do more or less of
in the way you start your day?

What's your Soul's sense of how you are beginning each morning?

Mystery Unfolding

If you knew
when it would end,
would you still
seize the day
and live as fully?

If you knew
that it would take a few jobs
to find your life's work,
would you be as engaged
in all your missions
of your unfolding purpose?

If you knew
how you'd meet your partner,
would you still love others
as deeply
helping you grow
and deepen your capacity to love
each lover along the way?

If you knew
the how and the when
of some of your major life events
would you still live
with the same curiosity and engagement?

Most would not
and so it's trickled down
from Soul to conscious mind
on a need to know basis.

It's okay though,
this by design,
helps you trust Life,
surrender to the process,
read the signs,

find your direction,
learn along the way
and embrace every moment of it.

"Despite knowing the journey and where it leads, I welcome it and embrace every moment of it"

| Arrival |

At the End of Your Days

On your deathbed,
how do you want to look back
and feel about your life?

Will you have rolled up your sleeves
and entered into the fray?
Will you have touched and tasted
the depth and range of life?

What would you have missed, not having done?
What would you regret, not having become?
What would the world have lost, had you not contributed?

Will you have allowed yourself
to feel and be felt,
see and be seen,
know and be known?

Will you have opened your heart,
allowing yourself to love and be loved,
learned compassion for others,
felt then depths of joy and sorrow?

On your deathbed,
how do you want to look back
and feel about your life?

Freedom in the Face of Death

From the moment of conception
Death is waiting in the shadows
dimly illuminated in the age of innocence,
with every lived moment
the nearer it gets to you.

What is this battle in the heart of Nature
vying with itself as Life eats Life?
Being so disconnected from the natural world,
we forget the natural cycles of living and dying.

The older we get, the closer it looms,
seemingly scary at first
so it's easier to deny its presence
and go through the motions of life.

Instead of integrating and celebrating,
we drug up the aging and put them in homes,
we institutionalize and hide away the dying,
getting distracted in our obsession with youth.

Perpetually avoiding our own fear of death,
blindly keeping alive as long as possible,
focusing more on denying and staving off,
than really living well and living fully.

The moment is uncertain, but the end is assured.
Life will consume us all one way or another.
It may come suddenly and swallow you whole
or break you down slowly, bit by bit.

You can't defeat the Grim Reaper's
specter of Death with procedures and potions.
You win by having left it all on the field;
to die well, is to have lived and loved well.

The depth of grief in losing someone,
is the reciprocal of how much you loved.
And this agony of grieving also
cracks your heart open to love more deeply.

Death teaches about love
to savor our limited time together,
fully loving while they're here
and letting go and grieving when they're gone.

But even more sad than the final breath
is "killing time" and wasting your life
or sacrificing what really matters, just to earn money
in hopes to have the freedom to do it later.

Do you know the greatest regrets
of people on their deathbed?
Worrying about the superficial things,
not having laughed more,
not expressing how they really feel,
fearing what others think instead of living authentically,
not having deeper connection with friends and loved ones,
and wishing they'd let themselves be happier.

The Agent of Death will come for us all;
the question is what will you do
between your birth and the final moment?

Be mindful of the *memento mori*:
"remember you must die".
It doesn't have to be a dark agent
breathing down your neck
and peering over your shoulder.
It can also be a great privilege,
the opportunity to live and love
taste and touch, experiencing
the depth and range of Life.

Knowing the last breath is inevitable
can inspire you to live fully.
Knowing it is a finite experience,
sensing the presence of time and death,
invites you to savor the present moment.

Instead of earning salvation or proselytizing
to mitigate your own fear of death,
or living in denial and pretending,
Embrace it.
The more you can become
fearless in the face of death,
the more fully you can live.

And so
since you're gonna be here
for some amount of time,
why not choose to make the most of it?
Use your life for the cultivation of virtue
the pursuit of truth, beauty and goodness,
being of service to something greater,
leaving it better than when you came in,
growing, loving, contributing and Awakening.

The physical substrates of your body
are actually ancient stardust
that has been changing forms for eons,
just as much dark matter as light,
part of a Universe vast and expansive,
like your Essence, two faces of the same coin.
Life and death are not opposites:
experience them both as sacred.

Life is trying to Wake you up
in the great game of becoming Aware of Itself.
What is it that is Aware of thought?
Awareness, more vast than your body.
Awareness, greater than identity.

Awareness, beyond time and space.
Awareness Itself, "your" True Nature,
the Field in which all things arise.
Some ego parts fear the unknown,
yet what if all this time
what you thought was the Grim Reaper,
was actually the Great Mystery
and facing the fear of death
has been a doorway into true Freedom.

Ultimately, Death comes for us all.
Don't miss the great opportunities it offers
to live fully and love deeply
with all your heart,
while surrendering wide open,
Awake in Life and Death.

How will you face your last breath?

Knowing its inevitability, how will you live?

The Ultimate Embrace

The more you embrace Death,
the deeper you can live Life.
Embrace Life as it arises
and it will not come
at you as an enemy.

Knowing you are
more than a body,
more than your thoughts,
more than a personal sense of self,
you can be free
in the face of death
without a worry of when
this current dance will end.

Remember,
you are
a unique Soul
that takes a body
to experience a life
while simultaneously
Awareness Itself.

Your Time is Limited

Your time is limited.
Don't waste it
chasing status
or objects you falsely think
mean something about you,
to bolster an ego
that is transparent anyway.

"You" are a Soul
here to learn, grow, love
and experience being alive.
So don't squander it
living someone else's "life".

Experience real life fully,
love deeply,
cultivate virtues,
contribute positively,
find peace and joy inside
live from the authenticity
of your Soul and
Awaken as Awareness.

"Your time is limited,
don't waste it
living someone else's "life".

| Steve Jobs |

The True Privilege

Can you feel the yearning
to know and be known,
to see and be seen
to listen and be heard
to feel and be felt
to love and be loved
in the depth and range
of your dynamic humanness
and the brightness of our Soul?

Can you feel the longing
to surrender open
allowing Grace to shine through
accepting as you be now
and in your further becoming,
wide Awake, as Awareness Itself?

This is the true privilege.

The privilege of a lifetime is being who you are.

| Joseph Campbell |

True Legacy

Before your last breath,
will you be more concerned
about what people thought of you or
how you impacted them?

For some, while living,
their primary focus is on *surviving*.
For others, it is on *taking*
what they can get from life and others
and raising their self-esteem.

But as you go higher up on Maslow's ladder,
some of you want to live fully,
grow and be a life-long learner,
open your heart, love deeply
and actualize your greater potential.

So, at the end of your days,
how will you have lived
and what impact
will you have had
on others and the world?

Will you have evolved your consciousness,
positively contributed your gifts
and used your life to make the world a better place?

In *your* final moments.
reflecting from a slow decline
or suddenly straight to the *Bardos*
how will others feel about
the ripple of your wake?

What do you want your true legacy to be?

Living Deeply

Learn and grow.
Heal your own past trauma.
Actualize your greater potential.
Cultivate virtues.
Contribute your unique purpose.
Enjoy your life.
Open to feel pleasure.
Thrive and live richly.
Live with an open loving heart.
Awaken Spiritually.

A life rippling outwards—
as a living legacy.

PART 2

GROWTH

Growing Bright

Sometimes the plant grows
toward the light
with a warm invitation,
from the Source, Sun.
Other times,
maturation is forced
by the stress of
crisis, chaos or challenge.

In the amnesia at birth
we forget why we're here.
From seed to tree,
embryo to actualization,
Life beckons us all
to grow and Awaken.

Follow the signs and synchronicities
becoming more conscious.
Utilize the support,
evolving and expanding.
Align with your tribe
walking each other home.
Keep growing brightening Soul,
going toward the light.

I Hope You Make the Best of It

Whatever phase of life you are in,
you can grow or stay the same.

It's never too early to get started.
And it's never too late to continue,
learning, growing, and healing,
working towards a better future
and becoming your greater potential.

Whatever hand you've been dealt,
I hope you will have played it well
at least by the end of this one.
You can make it better, or worse.

And if at some point, you don't like
the direction you are headed,
I hope you have the courage
to make a change, make it better
or start all over again.

What does "playing your hand well" mean to you and how can you live more in alignment with that?

SLOWLY THOUGH FORWARD

I began to listen to the whispers
beckoning me to grow.
I accepted the hero's quest
to follow forward on my path.
At my best and most alive,
when living at my edge of evolution.

I face challenges life presents
as opportunities to evolve.
I continue to persevere
in the face of obstacles.
When I get knocked down,
I get back up again.

I heal my past,
making space for my brighter future.
I open my heart,
ever-deepening my capacity to love.
Little by little, day by day,
cultivating my greater potential.

Awaken my Soul,
slowly though forward.

*This piece is inspired by the spirit of the song
"Slowly but Forward" by East Forest*

Remember When Waking

We are here
to learn,
to grow,
to enjoy,
to contribute
and Awaken.

But you are free
to go at your own pace,
stay asleep as long you like,
or get lost in illusion.
Repeat patterns until you learn,
or devolve into karmic debt.

The Universe is ancient
and has proven to be patient
with its growth
in matters of evolution.

So, when you are ready,
may your Soul remember
why you are here and
prioritize what matters.

This piece is inspired by the spirit of the spoken word "What to Remember When Waking" by David Whyte

The Pain of Waste

Change and uncertainty
can be scary,
but looking
back years later,
realizing you've stayed stuck
and haven't grown much,
is far more painful.

Expanding or Clinging

Live in the openness of possibility,
step forward into growth,
and expand into your greater potential.

Or cling to the safety of the known,
keep playing small
and stay stuck as you are.

Your choice.

What is an area of your life in which you are clinging to the past and what is an area in which you are expanding into your greater potential?

Growing or Going Through It?

Do you really want
to waste your life
going through the motions,
merely surviving,
or killing time?

Or do you want
to grow through life,
live fully,
love deeply
contribute your gifts
and make your life an offering
to something greater?

Ready to Grow

Growth is not guaranteed.

You can resist or distract yourself
for as long as you like.

Eventually the pain
of wasting your life
ultimately reaches
a tipping point
as you finally admit,
something has to change.

And, finally you are ready.

Lifeforces

Some pretend to be "fine",
going through the motions
numbing out with substances,
distracting with things that don't matter
or prioritizing self-esteem needs.

But Life wants you to grow.
So you can be proactive
and get started on your own
or wait for a catalyst
like crisis, pain, loss or illness—
Life's forces, forcing you to grow.

Are you more aligned with the forces of Life's evolutionary pull or making Life force you to grow?

Easier and Better

Life will challenge you to evolve.
The more you resist,
the more suffering it creates.

Engage in your evolution,
but remember,
it doesn't have to be all serious.

The more of the past you clear,
the more developed you grow,
and the more you open
to pleasure, joy and prosperity,
the easier the process gets,
the brighter you become,
and the better life can be.

How does it get even better than this?

On Growing and Becoming

Growing as a Soul
and becoming your greater potential
is part of why you are here.

You can have some parts
that are very developed and
others that are still young and maturing.

Development can be beautifully elegant and sexy,
or chaotically turbulent and grossly messy.
It can be rapid and powerful,
or slow and smooth,
magical and synchronistic,
or challenging and confronting.
as you bumble your way through infinity.

Growth may happen in a range of ways:
in a flash of insight or a moment of Grace,
learning practical new skills
or releasing past trauma,
through transition, upheaval and loss,
or after a long phase of intentional growth.

It may stretch you and expand you
thrusting you into new ways of being
or it can involve nuance and subtle integration
as you become more skillful, functional and masterful at life.

Whatever phase of growing you find yourself in,
remember that you can develop
at your own pace and process
in this beautiful and humbling
human experience
of growing, becoming and Awakening.

What is the Lesson?

You may not want
a certain thing
to be happening.
But it's not the first time,
you've faced this pattern.

Is it possible
this experience,
is a life lesson,
an unexpected teacher,
circumstantially sent
to help you grow,
cultivate virtue and
evolve your consciousness?

What is a recent life lesson you've been learning?

The Paradox of Change

At first, I didn't care
about much more than myself:
I really just wanted
more pleasure and less pain.

As I started to become more aware,
I tried to be more positive,
get physically healthy
surround myself with good vibes only
and manifest my best life.

And as I grew in empathy
I started to care more about others
and wanted to change the world,
until I started to realize,
I needed to be the change
I wished to see in the world.

As the deepening progressed
I started to heal and develop myself.
And as I grew, so too did my acceptance
of myself and the world.
Eventually, I no longer
needed to fix anything.

Out of this space
of acceptance and
surrendering of my will,
the instinct to evolve
re-emerged as the evolutionary instinct
of Life Itself to evolve
through me and the world.

So, as fixing became evolving,
it's come back full circle.
Full acceptance first,
absolutely perfect each moment,
while paradoxically ever-evolving.

Adulting

Adulting
is more than just
something you joke about,
because you fear
you'll lose your freedom
if you 'grow up'
or act responsibly.

Growing up
is an integrative process.
You can be both
a mature, aware adult
while also being joyful, alive and free.

Waking up and growing up.
Your Soul invites you
to become all of it.

*Adult human development is an evolutionary process
towards greater awareness, embodied integration,
perspective-taking, empathy, wisdom, joy, freedom and love
from the felt-sense foundation of Unified Oneness.*

So would you like to continue growing?

To the Wonder

How did you get so serious?
When did you stop playing
and having real fun,
without needing alcohol
to free you up?

When did you lose
the sense of wonder,
stop seeing the beauty
and disconnect from
the aliveness
of existence?

How can you be
a successful, responsible, aware adult,
and still be free,
deeply enjoying
the pleasure of your life
and the joy of being alive?

Here is how it can be done:
Release past trauma.
Do partswork to become free inside.
Allow more play and spontaneity.
Spend more time in nature.
Learn to be still and sense.
Open your heart to feel, feel it all—
the grief, the joy, the ache, the awe.

And there,
in the fullness of Being,
free of the past,
not worrying about future,
open in the Presence—
that's where wonder lives.

Can you still feel the wonder?

Personal Growth and Beyond

Personal Development,
might have begun for you,
as a way to ease suffering
or be more successful.

But if you keep going,
it evolves into
learning ways to relax,
becoming healthier
while connecting with tribe.

For the truly inspired,
who continue onward
it deepens into focusing
on healing and growing
as ways to embody
your greater potential
and contribute your purpose.

And for the very rare few
drawn further beyond,
the once very personal process,
transforms into the trans-personal—
meaning greater than the individual—
Awakening as Awareness Itself.

What is beyond your personal sense of self?

It's Been Her this Whole Time

And then one day,
we may realize
that all along,
throughout our entire lives,
during all the play and growing up,
all the testing and challenges,
all the achievements and accolades,
even all the ways
she has been asking us to grow,
were actually the Great She
the Divine Muse Herself.

She has been
inspiring us to grow and expand—
in Her many various forms,
our partners, parents,
teachers and mentors—
all inviting us to evolve
calling forth our greatness,
beckoning us beyond
comfort and convention,
to living our own hero's quest,
to awakening our greater potential,
to offering our lives in service
in positive contribution to the world
on behalf of all of us.

The very she we have been
dancing with all this time
is actually an emissary
of the Ultimate She,
seductively summoning us
to open, rise up and enter
in the giving of our greatness
to Life Itself.

//
PART **3**

Healing

The Way Beyond is Through

When you want to "get past this"
remember to feel and release it,
instead of trying to bypass it.
The way beyond is through.

The phrase "the way out is through", now a popular and widely used expression in its own right, is most often attributed to the poet Robert Frost based on his poem "A Servant to Servants" in which he writes:
"The only way to get rid of it
Was to get through it."

Your Body Keeps Score

Your body keeps score
of what was too overwhelming,
to feel fully at the time.

Perhaps you hadn't learned
enough emotional intelligence to self-regulate,
to feel, digest and release it yourself,
or didn't have the emotional presence
and co-regulation from your caregivers.

So, it's like the instincts of your body
did an override in saying
it might be better to suppress this now
and store this for a better time in the future
when you will be more able
to effectively feel and release it.

This piece is inspired by the spirit of the research and life of trauma expert, psychologist, professor and researcher Bessel van der Kolk in his best selling book "The Body Keeps the Score"

Wisdom in the Sensations

The seemingly uncomfortable
sensations in your body,
may be your subconscious
trying to communicate to you.

You can numb, distract and avoid
being present in your body,
as long as you want,
but the cost of ignoring
keeps you stuck where you are,
impoverishes your Soul,
and denies the greater wisdom
trying to guide and enhance your life.
These deadzones of unconsciousness
take up valuable space,
where joy, aliveness and peace
could be inhabiting you instead.

Or you can learn
to be still and sense,
presencing the messengers
listening and applying their wisdom,
then feeling and releasing them,
so you can stay open and free,
allowing the magic of Life
to live and flow through you.

For When You Are Ready

Your body
remembers trauma
and stores it for later,
until you are ready and able
to feel, digest and release it.
And it may eventually
attract similar situations
to remind you to heal
what you stored for later,
for when you are ready.

Your Pain and Potential

Your undigested past
is taking up valuable real estate.
Underneath the pain,
is your hidden power
and greater future potential.

Will you have the courage
to feel and release your past,
free your mind from limitation,
and rediscover the peace and joy
at the center of your being?

Will you clear the terrain,
the past pain and conditioning,
so you can build an amazing life,
with a brighter, freer future?

Little "T" Trauma

Trauma is not necessarily
what happened to you;
it's more like how you
interpret what happened
based upon your personality
and past undigested trauma load.
So, any feeling that is greater than
your capacity to stay present with,
feel, digest and release in the moment
gets stored as trauma,
to be processed later.

The Varieties of Wound Experiences

The wound is where the light gets in,
whether from trauma or karma,
whether it started with you or your lineage,
or whether it happened in this life or another.

If you'd like to feel and release
some of the undigested pain from
some of the challenges
you have previously experienced,
it's all part of the process
inviting your Soul to evolve,
by healing some of these wounds.

Healing is intertwined with
personal and spiritual growth
so here are some of your catalysts:

Specific Event Trauma—*personal*
emotional or psychological pain resulting from a particular, identifiable event in one's life, such as an accident, assault, interaction, words or other deeply overwhelming experience that was too intense or that you were unable to fully digest and release in the moment.

Missed Developmental Needs Trauma—*personal*
wounds or missing life skills that stem from unmet needs during crucial developmental stages in childhood. These can include lack of emotional support, protection, neglect, connection, attunement, abuse, etc., which can continue to impact a person's emotional and psychological well-being throughout their life.

Past Life Trauma—*soul / personal*
unresolved traumas from previous lifetimes can continue to affect a person in their current life, implying a continuity of consciousness across lifetimes.

Karmic Debt—*soul / personal*
karmic debt refers to the consequences of actions in this life or past lives that are believed to influence a person's present circumstances, implying a cycle of cause and effect that spans lifetimes.

Lineage Trauma/Karma—*family or ancestral*
trauma and its associated emotional patterns can be passed down through generations within a family. Research shows that ancestors' experiences can impact the emotional and even physical health of their descendants.

Collective Trauma—*cultural or species*
large-scale traumas experienced by entire groups of people, such as those caused by war, genocide, persecution, racism or natural disasters. These events can leave lasting emotional scars on a culture, race or even an entire species.

And all of these experiences
allow you to learn,
to deepen in wisdom,
to be more compassionate,
to respect of yourself and others,
to grow as a Soul,
and in these myriad ways
the crack of the wound
is where the light gets in.

"The wound is the place where the Light enters you."

| Rumi |

Why Is This Coming Up Now?

You were really starting
to feel stable
and doing well in your life;
why are these memories
coming up now?

Well that's how it works.
Those events and
the overwhelming feelings
were too much at the time,
so you suppressed them then,
saving it for a later time
when you would be
in a more resourced place in life
and have more emotional skills.

Your psyche wants you
to heal it eventually.
It's kind of like you took out
a trauma loan then,
but you are doing much better now,
so it is time to start repaying it.

Language of the Body

It's not about trying to
get rid of the feeling.

Sometimes,
it just needs to be felt
and after doing so,
it releases on its own,
without even knowing
what it was about.

Other times,
it needs to be felt and known
so it can reveal a message
to your conscious mind,
something important
to guide you,
to help you be more whole
and to improve your life.

And it speaks
in the language of the body
through sensations and emotions.

So won't you tune into it, feel and listen?

The way out is through.

Feel it fully,
until it releases
on its own
or dissolves
after being known.

Reassigning Protectors

Sometimes you just need
to give yourself permission
to feel something fully,
in order to release it.

Maybe it is as simple as
reminding yourself
that it's okay to feel.
Or maybe the protectors
you've used to keep you safe
by guarding your vulnerability
and avoiding feeling emotion
have been doing
such a great job,
but with their filters
turned up so high
they're keeping everything
locked up tight.

So if you're ready,
the next move is
to befriend them,
listen to them
and ask about their job,
appreciate and honor them
for their diligent efforts.

Then, when you are ready,
those protectors can be
given new operating orders,
with loving permission
to stand down and
relax off to the side.

So you can now learn
to feel and release
one emotion at a time.

This piece is inspired by psychological parts work as presented by Hal & Sidra Stone PhDs in Voice Dialogue and Dick Schwartz in Internal Family Systems.

Grieve Fully

Grieve fully.
Let yourself go through all the stages.
Don't mentally or spiritually bypass.
It's okay to feel the full spectrum.

You may be in shock, at first.
Maybe even denial and disbelief,
guilt about not doing things differently,
anger at yourself, others or Life,
bargaining for another chance
to make it better, to bring it back.
Then the depth of sadness really hits,
before full acceptance of what happened
and finally the upturn to a new future.

You'll know
you have finished grieving
when you can think about
the person or thing,
without a remaining emotional charge,
other than love and missing,
or clear insight and peace.

Grieving is one of Life's ways
of honoring something
you felt connected with and cared for.
Or acknowledging an experience
you regretfully missed out on.

If you don't allow yourself to grieve,
and feel and release all related emotions,
it will congest your heart,
inhibiting your present joy
and your future capacity to love.

If you do allow yourself to grieve,
fully engage the entire process
for weeks, months or however long you need,
you will have honored the grieved,
tended to your own heart
and become even more open and loving.

This piece is inspired by the Stages of Grief by psychiatrist Elisabeth Kübler-Ross who first introduced the concept in her 1969 book "On Death and Dying."

Soul Knowing

Your Soul knows
what to do to heal.
Your task is to either
get quiet and listen,
or work with someone
who can translate.

Heart Pull

Allow yourself to follow
the magnetic attraction
of your heart's deepest longing.

It will guide you to grow,
lead you to your purpose,
and draw you to your person*.

It will not lead you astray...
if your heart is open
and connected to your Soul.

If you don't do your inner healing, so you can listen and feel your own central heart it tends to be harder to hear its guidance towards a better future.

And in romance, if you go about it unconsciously, you might be led to to trauma bond(s), forcing you to heal and grow. For more information see the Imago work in Getting the Love You Want: A Guide for Couples by Harville Hendrix and Helen LaKelly Hunt.

So do your inner work, make peace with your past and repair your childhood unmet needs. Then, you can open your heart to giving and receiving even more love and, in doing so, your heart's pull will guide you to your best self, brightest future, and deepest capacity to love.

At Peace With the Past

To make peace with your past—
feel and release all emotional charge,
until, when you think about that event,
you feel relaxed, open and alive.

You can't just tell yourself to forgive,
or try not to think about it,
pretending it doesn't bother you.
You have to feel and release all the layers,
first the anger, hurt, and resentment
then maybe disappointment or sadness,
until when you think about the person or event,
you feel relaxed, open and alive.
Then you will have really forgiven.

It is in this free and open space
having released the stored baggage
of your previously undigested past,
now lighter, freer and clearer,
unconditioned by what once was,
available to co-create a brighter path.

Keep walking slowly forward,
doing your healing and releasing,
until you are at peace with the past—
open for the love to shine forth
and your future potential to live through.

The Source at the Center

Sometimes we forget
the Sun is always shining
even when past hurts
and undigested emotions
are covering our heart,
like clouds, seemingly obscuring
the light of the Central Sun
the Source of all Life
like the Love
that is the Essence
at the center of our Being.

PART 4

PURPOSE

Why Are You Here?

Why are you here?

Who are you here to be and become?

What are you here to do and contribute?

What do you care so deeply about
that you are willing to dedicate your life to
or give your life for?

One of the great tasks of your life
is to ask yourself these deeper questions.
and accept your own personal hero's quest
to discover the answers and
become the living embodiment
of your unique purpose.

What's Yours to Do?

What are your unique strengths and talents?

What limits and holds you back?

What blocks or blindspots get in your way?

What skills have you been developing?

What superpowers can you activate?

How do you feel inspired
to contribute to the evolution of our world
to making it even more
knowledgeable,
functional,
sustainable,
beautiful,
truthful,
ethical,
loving
&
Awake?

How to Live With Purpose

If you don't know your purpose, start with these:

HEALING: heal your past trauma and clear your karma.

GROWTH: learn life lessons, build skills, develop your potential, while cultivating virtue and wisdom.

PURPOSE: discover your purpose and contribute positively to the betterment of our world.

ENJOY: live deeply and fully savor the beauty, pleasure and joy of Life.

LOVE: deepen your capacity to give and receive love with yourself, others and Life.

AWAKENING: awaken as Non-Dual Loving Awareness Itself.

Living your purpose almost always involves your own Soul growth, so if you can't yet articulate your purpose or don't yet know how you want to contribute, start with your own healing and growth.

Living Your Purpose

Do you know your purpose
and are you living it?

How are you using
your precious human life
to positively contribute to our world?

Some are complacently contented
to stay asleep, avoid, numb out,
or go through the motions.
But a courageous few,
hear a deeper calling.

Life beckons us each
on our own epic hero's quest
of discovering and living
our unique life purpose.

It may begin as a quiet whisper,
or a dissatisfying frustration
with where you are now
and what you know is possible,
as Life's guidance creates
a series of circumstances
helping shift your course
and inviting you to follow the signs
leading you to the sense
that there's something more.

And the more you
accept the great quest of your life,
learn to quiet your mind,
listen to your inner compass
and trust the process
the more it will guide you
on each mission along the way.

Rise to the challenge,
discover your direction,
set your coordinates
each morning when you wake up,
align your life and decisions
and live your unique purpose,
contributing a beneficial ripple
for you, me and our world.

What is your "why",
your purpose in being here and how can you live it more fully?

This Instinct Inside You

There's this instinct
that lives
deep inside you.
It wants to
move though you,
to heal you,
to open you
and evolve you.

And there are moments,
along the way,
when other parts of you
may try to stop this process,
ignore its whispers,
slow things down,
keep things safe,
and stave off the unknown,
to avoid the stretching pains
of authentic growth.

So yes it takes courage.
And yet,
the more
you do follow it,
the more
it guides you,
the easier it gets and
the faster it goes.

But if you allow it,
It wants to free
the places that are bound,
love the places you don't yet love,
actualize your potential
and Awaken as something
much greater than one individual.

It has been calling you,
will you let it live through you?

Inspiration Not Insignificance

Don't allow the feeling
of insignificance
to stop you
from making a difference.
Do your inner healing
to release your
past trauma
and limiting beliefs
so your motivation
can be animated by inspiration
instead of the dirty burning fuel
of trying to prove yourself,
seeking validation
or feeling worthy of love.

Happiness and relaxation
are available to you now.
But, you have to
release your past,
learn to relax.
Don't delude yourself
into thinking you'll find them
in some future accomplishment:
they are living inside you now.

The place you'll find
happiness and relaxation
is the same space
your realize enoughness
and from there
the source of the
highest motivation,
the inspiration
to develop your potential,
contribute your purpose

and spiritually Awaken,
as you open yourself
to allow Life
to work, love and live
through you
toward a better, brighter
and more beautiful world.

Are the current motivations in your life more fueled by getting away from insignificance or animated by inspiration?

DEEP DEDICATION

What inspires you
so much
that you'd dedicate
your life to it?

What
do you care
so deeply about
that you'd give
your life for?

What are you dedicated to?

Aim High

Aim high—
remember why you are here.

Do what it takes to
embody your greater potential.

Upgrade your life
to match the standard of your Soul.

Collaboratively co-create
the more beautiful world
your heart knows is possible.

What limiting beliefs or fears are holding you back from aiming higher?

This piece is inspired by the books, essays and workshops of philosopher and futurist Charles Eisenstein.

Life Beckons You

Have you heard it calling you?

It may have started,
as a vague inner whisper,
easily drowned out
in a world of distractions.
Maybe because it is not so obvious
it makes it even that more special
for those who listen and follow it.
It's like this difficult to articulate,
yet gnawing sense,
that there has to be
something more
to life than this.

Little by little it captures
and calls you forward
as your searching gets stronger,
as you notice and value
the signs and synchronicities
and as you accept your purpose quest.

Persevere through the transitions,
engaging the lessons and challenges,
staying curious and engaged,
the more you are able to be present
within the emergent process,
and the more you realize
this inner beckoning
has been the reciprocal homing signal
attracting you forward all along
to learn and grow,
to discover and live
your unique purpose,
one mission at a time.

Purpose Prayer

Universe, grant me:

The **courage** to follow the calling and my unique path.

The **discernment** to get still and quiet,
to listen and sense the signs
and follow higher guidance.

The **resilience** to continue mission by mission,
discovering, developing and delivering
my unique purpose as a
positive contribution to our world.

This piece is inspired by the Serenity Prayer

PART 5

VIRTUE

Soul Uploads

Go ahead,
have all the experiences you want,
enjoy all the pleasure you desire,
accumulate as many possessions
as you can,
and manifest as much as you want,
but only the lessons you've learned,
the wisdom, virtues and love
come with you in the transition.

The thing about Souls
having a human experience,
is that no "body" gets out alive.
You don't take any "thing" physical with you,
after your last breath
in this dimension.

What does get uploaded
to the Soul cloud:
the trauma you've healed,
the karmic debt you've left unpaid,
the lessons you've learned,
the positive ripples you've contributed,
the virtues you've cultivated
the human codes you've embodied
and your open-hearted capacity to love,

Knowing that, how will you live?

Character Emanation

You reveal
the character
you've cultivated
by demonstrating:
your resilience
when you have little,
your gratitude
when you have a lot,
and your kindness
toward others
when you don't need
anything from them.

Respect

People treat you
the way you treat yourself.

If you want to be more respected,
start by respecting yourself.

Take responsibility for your life.
Do what you say you'll do.
Take care of yourself.

Stop doing the things that weaken you.
Make the best of what you have.
Take steps toward your greater potential.

Carry yourself with respect
and live a life you are proud of.

You'll walk the world with respect
and inspire others to do the same.

What are some ways you can respect yourself more?

GRIT

Not all smooth and shiny.

An inner strength
seasoned with character;
persevering in the face
of adversity and obstacles.

When the going gets tough,
grit fuels you to keep going,
when you get knocked down,
grit gets you back up again.

It is a tenacious determination
plus a growth mindset.
courageous resilience
with a thirst for betterment.

A measure of how you
deal with failure,
learn from your mistakes
and use them to keep improving.

Raw talent is good to start with,
but by itself might not yield much.
Talent plus practice builds skill,
and skill plus grit leads to mastery.

Be strong and hang tough.
Stay committed and carry on.
Live with heart.
Cultivate grit.

Less of This, More of That

Stop doing
the things
that make you feel
weak,
small
and
separate.

Do more of
what makes you feel
present,
confident
and
loving.

And do more of
what makes the world
better,
brighter
and more
beautiful.

What are some things you do that make you feel weak?

What are some things you can do to be more virtuous?

Embodiment

You can read all the great books,
listen to the top podcasts,
travel to retreats in exotic lands,
wear the hippest woo-woo clothes,
and rattle off the new age lingo,
until your puffy lips turn blue.

You may know some spiritual concepts,
but when a quality is truly embodied,
it emanates through your presence,
so people can feel it when you speak
and sense it through your body
as you move through the world.

*Can you apply it
in a real life situation
when it really matters?*

Skillfulness

Skillfulness:
is a dedication to cultivation
and the pursuit of self-mastery,
beyond mere technical talent,
for the inherent joy of learning,
acting with awareness and alignment
in the approach of excellence,
as a noble offering to Life Itself.

*In Japanese, this concept can be translated as "Shugyō"
or the practice of self-cultivation.*

Precision

In your distortion,
you are perfectionistic and obsessive,
rigid and attached to the one right way.

And in your virtue
you can execute with excellence
and see things with nuance,
with deep appreciation for detail.

Precision.

Sovereignty

Sovereignty of Attention
I am free to choose what I focus on and what information I consume, setting boundaries when needed and being intentional and mindful with my attention.

Sovereignty of Thought
I am free to think critically and systemically, use discernment, and think for myself: examining limiting beliefs, social constructs and ways of knowing that may have unconscious biases.

Sovereignty of Body
I am free to be in my body, move freely and dynamically, listen to my body, feed it vital nourishing foods, maintain natural health and make informed decisions, freely choosing what I put in my body without coercion from others.

Sovereignty of Emotion
I am free to fully feel, digest and release my emotions. I am interdependently connected to others, while being individuated without being codependent, allowing them to have their own identity, emotional state, and well-being as distinct from my own.

Sovereignty of Wealth
I am free to build diversified wealth, save wisely, invest wisely, leverage debt wisely, have an emergency fund and continually increase my financial intelligence and autonomy.

Sovereignty of Time
I am free to use my time as I feel inspired on things that foster and sustain my well-being, growth, enjoyment and positive contribution to the world.

Sovereignty of Natural Rights
I am free to understand, assert, protect and live in alignment with the inherent rights I possess as a birthright by being human. I recognize where I have autonomy and exercise my right to freedom of thought, speech, and self-determination without infringing on others.

What are some practical ways in which you could embody more sovereignty in your life?

Discernment

Sensing when to patiently wait and trust the timing, versus when to take action and seize the moment.

Sensing when to cautiously play it safe, versus when to boldly take a risk.

Sensing when to allow it to come to you, versus when to move toward it.

Sensing when to stay committed, versus when to walk away.

Sensing when to speak, versus when to stay silent and listen.

Sensing when to express vulnerability, versus when to keep it to yourself and not overshare.

Sensing when to advocate for your perspective, versus when to value both while agreeing to disagree.

Sensing when to say "yes" to an opportunity, versus when to say "no" to stay focused on your priorities.

Sensing when to trust your intuition, versus when to seek external guidance.

Life is not always as simple
as some make it seem,
but the more integrated
and discerning you become
the more your interactions
become smooth and skillful.

Learn to sense,
and cultivate discernment.

What is an area of your life in which you can be more discerning?

Higher Guidance

There is a part of you that knows:
how to protect and keep you safe,
when to patiently wait or take action,
and the direction toward your purpose.

This higher wisdom
has been inside you all along,
waiting for you
to become aware of it.

The more you listen
and trust your inner knowing,
the clearer it guides the way
to a life of purpose, virtue and love.

How do you cultivate this connection with your inner wisdom and higher guidance? (journaling, meditation, somatic therapy, nature, learning to trust yourself, or other spiritual practices)

Wisdom Wanting to Speak Through You

There a wisdom
that wants to speak through you.

It doesn't pose or posture.
And it doesn't beg to be heard.
Sometimes, it's just for you, to guide your life,
other times, it's for sharing, to help others.

It might be,
eloquent and profound,
clear and concise,
or only what's needed.

The more developed and integrated you become,
the more silent and still you are,
the more the wisdom can
guide and speak through you.

Intentional Flow

Planning is useful,
but rigid plans
can stifle the magic.
Intention is powerful,
but attachment to outcomes
can inhibit possibility.

Harness the clarity of intention
and the direction of planning,
while being adaptable.
Then breathe into
the heart of uncertainty,
relaxing and surrendering,
letting things unfold.

Learn to surf the emergent aliveness
of the adventure that is your life,
trusting the Universe,
in co-creating with
the power of Life.

Do you struggle with overplanning and rigidity? Or can your life benefit from harnessing the power of intentionality?

"Planning is essential; plans are useless."

| Dwight Eisenhower |

Manifesting

Set a clear intention.
Be grateful for what you already have.
Release any tension, blocks or fears
that could inhibit it from actualizing.
Relinquish attachment to outcomes.
Maintain your state high.
Focus on it every day.
Vividly visualize it,
feeling as if it is already here,
as you and Life together
co-create the emergent future.

Joyful Contagion

Relax open your heart,
allowing it to fill with so much joy
it effortlessly shines through,
as you move through the world,
without needing others to be
any different than they are
or having your happiness
dependent on others' state.

Your smile, your laugh
the radiance of your being,
your joyful contagion,
infectiously igniting
their own inner spark
so the joy at the center of Life,
like a glowing ember of aliveness,
starts to radiate from them too.

In psychology, the phenomenon of emotional contagion describes the way we can emotionally impact and influence those around us, whether one on one or in a group. The name alludes to the way we can "catch" emotions from others and underlies empathy, the vibe of the room, the emotional experience of a group, and the way a smile can be infectious.

Embodied Presence

I may hear it,
when you say it.

I'm more likely to see it,
when you do it.

But I can feel it most,
when it emanates
from your presence.

"We convince with our presence"

| Walt Whitman |

The Ascendant Bow

Bowing down
with
human humility.

Standing upright
with
Divine pride.

WISE AND LOVING

May your mind
be quiet
so your actions
can be guided by wisdom.

May your heart
be open
so your life
can be animated by love.

The Giving of Your Greatness

There is an indescribable joy of aliveness,
being filled and fueled by inspiration,
nobly accepting the call
of your own hero's journey
going toward your best self,
actualizing your potential
contributing your gifts,
living your unique purpose
free in the midst of it all
in the giving of your greatness
to Life Itself.

PART 6

EVOLUTION

Whispers From the Future

Like whispers from the future
calling your forward and deeper,
with vague visions of possibility
and soft Soul-stirring inner voices,
your future self invites you
to expand and Awaken
into your greater potential.

The Evolution of Life on Planet Earth

Cosmic Origins
originally from ancient star dust that has been changing forms for billions of years.

Planet Formation — *4.5 billion years ago*
a planet we call Earth was formed.

Tool Evolution — *2.5 million years ago*
tools were invented that radically enhanced hunting and food preparation.

Fire Evolution — *800,000 years ago*
the use of fire began and by 300,000 years ago fire was used on a daily basis which drastically reduced eating time from 5 hours to 1 hour.

Migratory Evolution — *70,000 years ago*
homo sapiens began exploring the planet by migrating out of Africa.

Cognitive Evolution — *70,000-35,000 years ago*
a genetic mutation occurred in homo sapiens, but not other species, creating a cognitive enhancement that allowed the species to proliferate by dramatically improving communication, cooperation and hunting.

Agricultural Evolution — *12,000 years ago*
By saving, planting and cultivating seeds, homo sapiens discovered they could grow agriculture which allowed the wandering nomads to settle into towns and villages which sparked the beginning of irrigation, food surplus, increased trade and specialized division of labor.

Scientific Evolution — *450 years ago*
The emergence of modern science began with developments in mathematics, physics, astronomy, biology

and chemistry, which led to transformations in world-views and inventions that reshaped our physical reality.

Industrial Evolution — *250 years ago*
Innovations in machine tools in mechanized factory systems combined with the inventions of the central water wheel and steam engines radically increased power, production and population growth.

Digital Evolution — *70 years ago*
The shift from mechanical and analogue to digital electronics ushered in the Information Age with sweeping technological changes brought about by computers, microprocessors, mobile cellular phones, and the Internet.

The Next Evolution — *now*
Genetic enhancement, virtual and augmented reality, Artificial Intelligence, robotics, automation, spirituality, block-chain, new economic and socio-political structures will momentously transform how we work, live, travel, acquire knowledge, communicate, and manage our health.

99% of all species to live on this planet have become extinct

How will you participate in the evolution of Life on Planet Earth?

*Alternate Timeline Theory — Graham Hancock's Perspective. Hancock's research challenges the mainstream view of human history, proposing that an advanced civilization existed more than 12,000 years ago and was wiped out by a cataclysmic event—likely a comet impact and/or flood at the end of the last Ice Age. He suggests that survivors of this lost civilization shared their knowledge of agriculture, architecture, and astronomy with early human societies, influencing the rise of ancient cultures like the Egyptians, Sumerians, and Mayans. His work, featured in Ancient Apocalypse *and supported by significant archeological and geological evidence, while controversial amongst mainstream historians, argues for a re-examination of current historical timelines.*

Ashes to Ashes, Stardust to Dust

The physical substrates
that make up your body,
the chemistry of the air you breathe,
the microscopic molecules of your cells,
the trillions of bacteria and viruses living on and in you,
were all forged billions of years ago
in the center of ancient stars.

Bright stellar glows burning out
in supernova explosions,
cosmic death and rebirth,
scattering into stardust
across the Universe
forming new stars and planets
with the same elements now in you.
From stellar ashes to ashes,
from stardust to dust.

Your mind may think
you are an isolated island,
separate from others
and the world.
But at every level of your being,
you are made of the same stuff
which connects to everything else.

What is the Source of all this?

Great Mystery,
vast Emptiness and dark matter
out of which everything
emerges and returns,
the same Aliveness
that animates all things,
evolving over eons

organizing Itself into forms
living, growing and dying,
arising and falling away,
seemingly islands
yet One Cosmic Ocean.

The Evolutionary Impulse

What are You
that animates
this urge in Life to evolve,
for galaxies to create stars,
the Universe to expand,
this creative light,
that shines through us,
learns through us,
that births through us
and is evolving through us?

The Great Chain

Even if you don't become famous,
you are still an essential link,
a part of the larger whole,
as indispensable as any other
in the Great Chain of Being.

Free yourself from your past,
learn, grow and evolve,
be loving and compassionate,
contribute something positive,
leave our world better and brighter
than you found it when you entered—
a noble offering to Life Itself,
the Great Chain of Being.

The concept of "the great chain of being" was explored by Arthur O. Lovejoy in his 1936 book of the same name. Lovejoy examined the historical development of this comprehensive worldview, tracing its roots back to the philosophies of Plato, Aristotle, and Plotinus.

Come Together

We are on a critical path
and these next hundred years
are a crucial time for
the extinction or evolution
of our human species.

Let us remember
we are on the same team
in this evolutionary process,
here on Spaceship Earth.

May we stop wasting
so much energy
fighting each other
and polluting our planet.

Let us come together
to generate creative solutions
to our world's most important issues
as we continue evolving into a
more sustainable, compassionate,
just and thriving world for us all.

*This piece is inspired by the spirit of the life's work
of Buckminster Fuller, architect, systems theorist, author, designer,
inventor and futurist (1895–1983).*

Seven Generations

Stop squabbling over
the details of climate change,
the "science" vs the conspiracies,
and keep the focus on what really matters.
Let's start living more sustainably.

I invite you to
expand your awareness
beyond just yourself,
to be considerate of others
and all life on this planet now
and seven generations into the future.

We are all inextricably connected.
May you and we increasingly Awaken
to this felt sense realization.

The Native American concept of Seven Generations is a powerful philosophy that emphasizes the interconnectedness of past, present, and future. It is believed to have been articulated by Iroquois Haudenosaunee whose Great Law of Peace emphasizes the importance of considering the impact of decisions on the next seven generations. It's a systemic way of thinking that encourages individuals and communities to consider the long-term consequences of their actions, not just for themselves, but for those generations who will come after them.

Humanity in the Age of Technology

We find ourselves alive
at a unique time
in this Digital Age
here on Planet Earth.
But when technological growth
outpaces human moral development,
it presents us with many new challenges
and considerations
in terms of ethics, privacy, health, parenting,
and philosophy of life.

As technological advancement
continues to accelerate,
we can further environmental degradation,
while fragmenting presence,
reducing real human connection
and decreasing happiness.

Or we can leverage technology
to increase sustainability,
enhance the standard of living,
and enrich our lives
with more time
for creativity, growth,
freedom and bliss.

May we continue
to integrate technology
into our world and lives
with awareness and consideration
in healthy ways
that enhance our lives
and this planet,
while still maintaining
our essential humanity
and intimate relatedness
to ourselves; each other;
the natural world
and Presence Itself.

What Will You Do Then?

It is possible
in your lifetime
that humans
on a mass scale
could have all
essential needs met:
food, warmth, shelter and
a universal basic income.

What if you
didn't have to devote
so much of your life
to survival and self esteem—
foundational needs?

What will you do
if you don't have to work
a job you don't like
to buy things
you don't need?

What then,
will you do with your
time, energy and attention?

How will you use your time?
What will you create?
How will you contribute?
How will you grow your Soul?

Even though a new tomorrow is near,
with AI, robotics and automation
on pace to transform this world,
you don't have to wait.

How will you use
your precious human life,
now and in the future?

Evolutionary Cultivation

Throughout human history
most were just trying to survive,
others sought safety and comfort,
accumulation for themselves
or self-esteem and status.

An extraordinary few
have dedicated their lives
to the cultivation of virtue
and the embodiment
of greater potential
wearing grooves of possibility
for future humans to come
and the evolutionary betterment
of life on this planet.

How will you use your life?

Span of Awareness

Part of evolving as a human
is becoming more self-aware
and more aware of the world.

But it takes some development
to have the capacity
to attend to much more
than our own physical survival
and self-esteem needs.

The level of stress and overwhelm,
in most of our daily lives,
inhibits many of us humans
from being able to
look and genuinely care
much beyond our own skin.

As we build our resources
and resourcefulness,
sort out the foundational levels,
we can deepen our care
and expand our span of compassion,
with increasing awareness
of ourselves, others and the world.

May we be inspired
to evolve enough
to expand our awareness,
beyond just ourselves,
as we each in our own way
help steward humanity
in its evolution
toward a better future.

Receiver of the Future

Release your lower mind
and its fixed ideas
of what has been,
the rigid right way,
or what is impossible.

Allow your higher mind
with its energetic antenna
to feel into the future
and be a receiver
of new possibilities
and novel innovations
to evolve our world.

Are you here to be an instrument of change and an embodied exemplar through which creative emergence is evolving our world?

PART 7

WAYSHOWERS

Explorers of Experience

For millennia,
the curious and courageous,
have explored the
depth and expanse of
the human experience.

Travelers ventured out,
discovered new places and
mapped the material terrain,
over land and sea and air.

Scientists experimented,
observing and understanding
our bodies and the natural world,
from ecosystems to the quantum.

Astronomers and astronauts
charted the outer reaches,
calculated cosmic forces and
journeyed into the darkness of space.

And Mystics explored
the inner dimensions of consciousness,
embodying universal wisdom and
elucidated the perennial philosophy.

We stand on your giant shoulders,
the great pioneers and cartographers
who have mapped and illuminated
the way forward for the evolution
of Life on planet Earth.

Ripples of Betterment

May the impact of your life,
the effectual emanation of your
words, actions and choices,
be a noble offering
of beauty, truth and goodness,
creating positive ripples
for the betterment of our world.

Keep Going Towards the Light

Keep going
towards the light
until you become
the Source
of that
which you seek.

Luminaries

The deeper you go
the brighter it can get.
And as you Awaken and thrive,
in the radiance of your overflow,
Life inspires others through you.

Glory Smiling Through

One person,
sees an animal dying
and looks away
from the cycle of Life,
unable to face
the stroke of death.

Another person,
sees that same animal
and feels first,
the sadness of loss,
then the glory of Grace
lovingly smiling through.

Ambassadors of Love

When our hearts are closed,
we can't feel the Love
that lives through all things.

Fortunately, there are beings
whose hearts are so open,
they allow the Love,
that is the essence of Life,
to shine and flow through.

We celebrate the
Ambassadors of Love,
whose capacity to live
with an open heart
naturally inspires
and permissions others.

Like contagious candles
igniting the latent love-light
within our hearts
sourced at the center of Existence,
illuminating, one by one,
until the whole world,
is bright Awake.

*or at least those who are ready or want to begin Awakening.

Pointing Others to the Light

If the Ultimate,
has already been realized,
but you came back again
to help others find their way,
thank you.

bodhisattva *n.* (Buddhism)
A person who has attained prajna, or Enlightenment, but who postpones Nirvana in order to help others to attain Enlightenment: individual Bodhisattvas are the subjects of devotion in certain sects and are often represented in painting and sculpture.

Path Carvers

Inspiring leaders and guides,
the ones who've gone ahead
to boldly walk the uncharted path,
mapping the terrain of new paradigms,
and embodying it first,
to pave the way
in stewarding others
to greater possibilities.

Mystics of the Ages

Mystics of the ages,
who directly feel
the presence of Oneness,
reminding us of
the deeper dimensions
and greater forces
inspiring and guiding
all our lives beyond
the daily dramas.

Mystics of the ages,
evolutionary exemplars and
beacons of brightness,
who illuminate our way,
embodying timeless wisdom
as ambassadors of our potential.

Humanity thanks you.

It's Safe This Time

To all those who've come before,
and dedicated your lives
to the healing, developing
and Awakening
of consciousness
on planet Earth.

To all those who've come before,
who in various times have been
persecuted, tortured and killed
as healers, visionaries and mystics.

To all those who've come before,
thank you for your brave service,
amidst all the suffering you've endured,
as part of this evolutionary process.

To all those who've come before;
we now bear the eternal torch
you've carried for so many millenia.
And because of all your precious work
in evolving our world,
we get to serve and thrive this time.

To all those who've come before,
it's safe this time.
We don't have to hide
or hold back anymore.
This is what we've been working towards;
preparing for a time like now.
We've finally reached the threshold,
and it's safe this time.

To all those who've come before,
it's safe this time,

so let's continue to do
what we came here to do,
shining brightly,
sharing our gifts,
fearlessly living our missions,
while being truly supported.
and have a lot of fun
doing it together.

It's safe for your soul to be fully seen
shining as brightly as possible
in sharing your gifts and helping humanity heal, develop & Awaken.

Stay Bright and Upright

During turbulent transformative times
full of fear, control and suppression,
when many have lost their way,
may you remember why you are here.

Stay aligned and sovereign,
think critically and be discerning,
take responsibility for your health,
stand tall and shine brightly,
as you courageously lead
and light the way forward,
ushering in a better world for us all.

A tribute to those who were clear and lived courageously in 2020.

Leadership in Times Like Now

Although many
of those around you
are confused, afraid,
or have lost their way,
some of you were born
for times like these.

Some have been been here before
paving the way for lifetimes,
others came backwards to now,
for this special phase in time,
as leaders and guides,
courageously stewarding
the positive evolution
of our world.

We've reached a critical mass;
the collective is ready.
Remember why you came.
Do what's yours to do:
inspired by something greater
guiding our way forward.

EVOLUTIONARY EMISSARIES

Some are here,
to embody the universal codes
of greater human potential,
as cosmic emissaries
in service to something greater,
to the evolution of consciousness,
as exemplars of possibility
for Life on Planet Earth.

While some individuals are naturally drawn to be public figures and influencers this time around, the vast majority of us contribute to positive change in quieter, more personal ways. In a multitude of micro-moments— small acts of kindness, conscious parenting, healthy choices, personal growth and positive work—we can each help lay the building blocks of a better world. Large or small acts all contribute to our individual evolution and, collectively, the evolution of society. This is a reminder that everyone has the potential to be a positive influence, each in our own way.

THAT WHICH LIVES THROUGH YOU

Thank you
for who you are,
for all you do.
Thank you
for allowing Life
to express through you
in ways that
touch,
move,
inspire,
empower,
embolden
and
ignite others.

Living Legacy

Learn and grow.
Heal your own past trauma.
Actualize your greater potential.
Cultivate virtues.
Enjoy life and experience pleasure.
Contribute your unique purpose.
Live with an open loving heart.
Awaken Spiritually.

A life rippling outwards—
as a living legacy.

To The Mystics and Wayshowers

To the mystics and wayshowers
across cultures and throughout time,
the trailblazers and torchbearers
who have illuminated our way,
secretly advancing
what is possible for our world.

To the scientists dismissed as heretics,
inventors who had their work destroyed,
the healers who were killed as witches,
yogis who were forced to live in caves,
the qi masters who trained in the mountains
and sages who taught in secret.

To all those who had to practice in hiding,
were imprisoned, persecuted or killed
because the masses were not ready
to receive their mission and transmission.

To all those who have come before
who have positively participated
in the maturation of our species
throughout the evolution of life
on this amazing planet Earth.

To those brave souls across the ages,
inspired by a deeper purpose,
who have used their precious lives
to prime the pathways of potential
for a time in the future
when our world would be more ready.

And as we usher in this next epoch,
may we utilize technology,
not for more distraction, escape or manipulation,

but integrate it with
wisdom, ethics, heart and presence,
to co-create emergent solutions
to our greatest collective challenges.

To the mystics and wayshowers
the giants on whose shoulders we stand,
the groove-wearers of potential
who courageously devoted their lives
to the healing, development
and Awakening of humanity.

May that same essential Grace
that inspired and lived through them
continue to guide our way,
Awakening and evolving through us
in creating a more loving,
empowered, sustainable,
thriving world for us all.

Gratitude & Acknowledgements

Thank you to all those who have expanded my mind, opened my heart, activated my body, brightened my Soul and inspired my life, past, present and future.

Special thanks to Matt Kreinheder, William Potter, Pete Kirshmer, Alex Regalbuto, Allen Bittaker, Jason Hernstad, Carole Griggs, Laura Styler, Cedric Winterwolf, Krista Richards, Josh McMurtrie, Apryl Stephenson, Michele Rooney, Dorothy Mandel, Koichi Naruishi, Caroline Mayou, James Cruzen, Josh Macin, Jess Magic, James Applington, Viraja Prema, Josh Trent, David Beaudry, Siatnee Chong, Fernando Mercado, Willow Brown, Kai Van Bodhi, Izzy Ivy, Chris Maher, Guy White, Lauren Peters, Tobin Wolfe, Aaron Moon, Andrew Reed, Shiloh Boss, James Fairman, Daniel Bradley, Keri Nola and Jeffrey Platts for your friendship and all the epic consciousness enhancing conversations.

Gratitude to Raina DeLear, Annalisa Aldeberg, Frank Carucci, Thomas Hubl, Dustin Diperna, James Baye, Laura Divine, Joanne Hunt and Bonnie Grossman for your wisdom, inspiration, healing and guidance.

Thank you Anastasia Smith, Drisana Carey, Komala Saunders, Sonia Reece, Sarah Speers, Kat Muller, Niki Van Houten and Katrina Carroll for your heartfelt devotion, help and service.

Thank you to my family, Mom, Vern, Jordie, Shannon, Beckett, Bronson, Dad, Valeta, Michael, Aubrey, Nani, Vernon Sr., for your consummate love, laughter and support.

And ultimately, thank you to all the mystics and wayshowers who have contributed to the evolution of consciousness on planet Earth.

To Awakening & service,

Johnny

ABOUT THE AUTHOR

MY RISING

I was a pretty typical kid growing up but at 16 years old a single experience began to dramatically shift the trajectory of my life. I have learned that we can have life altering tragedies or synchronistic blessings such as a flash insight, a "chance" meeting or a single profound sentence that can serve as powerful pivots in our life direction. I also know that consistently engaging in small actions over time, alter our course quite profoundly.

Have you ever experienced anything that shifted the course of your life either drastically in an instant or slightly, incrementally over time?

For me, a profound experience graced my path at 16 years old, while driving to school one day on a dusty, backcountry road. Suddenly, the entire moment relaxed open profoundly, like a vast seamless unity, in what seemed like a silent eternity beyond time. Then in a clear, deep, unwavering voice, a sound not localized in any place, said *"Have no fear of death, the body is just a vessel, you have a mission."* And then 30 seconds later, just as quickly as it opened to infinity, the scene collapsed back into the high school boy driving down the road. Yet, the afterglow endured through my young body, circulating with subtle tingles of aliveness, magnitudes greater than I had ever felt before. Partially elated, and also very shocked, I pulled over to the dirt shoulder and wandered into the natural landscape nearby. I fell to my knees in humility and profound curiosity about what had just transpired. Later, in the mind's search for meaning, I began reading a variety of religious, spiritual and philosophical books from various cultures and traditions. With newfound depth, curiosity and widening perspectives, Life progressively steered my trajectory beyond typical teenage boy concerns.

After high school, I studied Business Management Consulting at a University in Los Angeles, an hour and a half from home. Yet, it felt like I was living a dual life, unable to integrate what seemed like polar opposites. On one hand, I was a conventional teenager studying, socializing, partying and dating, and on the other hand, I was a secret depth seeker and explorer of possibility.

This continued even into working in Management Consulting in downtown Los Angeles on the conventional "road to success". Yet, some part of me noticed that, despite their relative "success", many middle-aged people I was surrounded by were not happy and lacked a deeper sense of purpose. And I continued asking the deeper questions of *"Why are we here?" "How are we to best live?" "What does true happiness feel like?"* I continued with these deeper contemplations, increasingly examining societal constructs and questioning my own inner assumptions.

Have you ever sensed there was something more and asked some of these deeper questions?

After work one clear, summer evening in my early 20's, while sitting on my balcony watching the sunset after work, I mused into the horizon *"There has got to be more to life than this."* Just a few months later, after this deeper inquiry, an unexpected back injury was the catalyst required for admittance into the next level of the Matrix. As a result of this injury, I was unable to sit for more than a short period and basically had to stand all day long as I tried to continue to work and live a "normal" life.

After more than a year of semi-functional living, standing all the time with limited function and continuous low-level pain, I was not improving. Despite diligent, but ineffective physical therapy, I was not improving. So, I opted for an experimental surgery, which failed and actually made things much worse. The "experimental" procedure ultimately had a short-lived trial period, because it was not only ineffective, but made many patients, like myself, much worse.

Prior to the surgery, I had difficulty sitting for more than 30 minutes, but I worked within the limitations, doing the best I could and was still relatively functional in my life. In fact, with a combination of ingenuity and necessity, I became an early adopter of the stand-up desk at work. But after the botched surgery, I became floor-ridden for the next two years, unable to stand for more than 5 minutes at a time. During the first, and worst, five months after the procedure, I was laid down on the floor for 22 hours a day. I was in so much pain that I didn't want to feel my body or emotions. Very humbled and unable to take care of myself, I moved back home with my parents.

At first, I resisted, *"Woe is me...why is this happening...what did I do to deserve this..."*. But after a few days, I realized that a negative attitude only made things worse—toxifying my inner state and being a downer for others around me. In the midst of the initial shock and pain, I had forgotten that I had been asking the Universe to give me the red pill in asking: "Is there more to life than this...". So, I decided to shift my perspective and make the best of the situation.

How would you feel if you had to spend 22 hours a day flat on the ground in intense pain? Would you wallow in sorrow or try to heal and rise up?

My physical body and location were very limited, to the point some would have considered it an imprisonment. I left my childhood home not more than ten times in an entire year, mostly to go to the doctor. However, in some ways I actually become more free internally. Firstly, I realized that no matter what my external circumstances, I had power over my attention and perspective. Secondly, I now had an abundance of time. I remembered all of the moments in the past when I wished I had had more time.

I made the most of that time, spending my days meditating, reading books, learning a foreign language, and watching a classic movie each night (as a healthy reward). I was most inspired by The Count of Monte Cristo, in which the lead character, who is wrongfully imprisoned, trains, learns and makes the best of his limited circumstances.

What would you do with all that "free" time?

Initially only able to walk short distances, I began taking walking breaks, gradually increasing the frequency and duration, as my body became stronger and able to stand longer. I went from being able to stand for five minutes and walk 100 yards, to being able to stand for 30 minutes and walk one mile at a time over the course of a year. Yet I was still in too much pain, unable to sit and not fully recovered. Though I had been making the best of the situation and had physically improved, progress was still too slow, and amidst frustration, confusion and doubt I wondered if I would ever get better.

I had been continuing to seek the advice of a leading spinal doctor in Southern California, who recommended that I have a disc fusion surgery. In his worldview, the surgical knife was the only thing that "might" make it better. However, part of me wondered if this was the best solution. I asked for guidance and greater clarity through prayer.

After a visit to an additional spinal specialist for a second opinion, who also suggested a second spinal surgery, I was synchronistically connected with an eccentric older man. This man, who became a wise ally, encouraged me to take full responsibility for my situation. He inspired the possibility in me that I could heal my body, instead of passively relying on drugs and surgery to fix me. I was a little skeptical at first, but I committed to giving it a try.

The first day, I actually vomited up green bile as the journey to purify my body and past had begun. For the next ten days, I strengthened and stretched my body for hours a day, morning until night. I felt like a combination of Luke Skywalker in the swamp with Master Yoda in Star Wars, soaking up new information like a sponge mixed with the disciplined training of an Olympic athlete. In this hyper-speed transformation of my mind and body, I made so much progress that I canceled the surgery and moved up to the Bay Area in Northern California to continue healing with newfound hope. Though I would be entering an unfamiliar world, I had crossed the threshold and never looked back.

The next 18 months proved to be an intense period of training, healing, learning and development. Determined to fully recover, I was open to trying almost anything. I learned to become more aware of and relax my body, including paying attention to how my body responded to different foods. I engaged in many different embodiment practices (stretching, weight-training, healthy eating, breath awareness training, progressive relaxation, biofeedback, qi gong, tai chi, yoga, somatic experiencing, trauma desensitization, etc.) and awareness practices (meditation, mindfulness, journaling, reading, and developmental coaching).

One day while wandering into a new health food store for the first time, I magnetically gravitated toward the back into a small room that seemed to be holding a lecture that had the participants captivated. As I curiously sat down, I realized the topic was natural vision improvement. It resonated because I had been severely near-sighted and wore thick glasses since I was eight months old when pneumonia, 105* fever and seizures disturbed my vision. I sat with rapt attention as the confident, inspiring speaker described his own personal step-by-step vision improvement process, as well as the successful, documented cases of numerous others. Once again, here was someone else inspiring me with the awareness that more was possible. Beaming with excitement, I returned home, and made a vow that very night to naturally improve my vision so that I would no longer need contacts or thick glasses.

There were plenty of naysayers along the way: optometrists who said it was impossible and family members who fearfully told me *"That's not possible. Put your glasses back on, you are going to go blind"*. But I knew it was possible. I stood in unwavering belief and used their doubt as fuel for my own determination. I dedicated 30 minutes a day to eye exercises and went to a progressive behavioral ophthalmologist for two hours a week to restore natural vision. Fifteen months later, and 24 prescriptions of glasses reduced, I passed optometrist and DMV visual exams with 20/20 vision. This marked the transformation of, not only my physical eyes, but symbolized my new capacity to see the world with more clarity and depth.

What originally began as an impetus to heal my back, sit without pain, be functional, work, and enjoy life became something much greater. I began aligning with a deeper motivation to actualize my potential, my unique gifts and bring them back into the world as a contribution of service. While I had been training the physical and mental parts of myself, in order to allow that deeper motivation to fully express itself, I would now venture into new arenas.

The next level of the training was in the interpersonal realm of connection and relating. Of course, from the outside I obviously interacted "normally" with friends, family and a series of girlfriends, but I had been unaware of the deeper human potentials of relating. Most of my life, I was so afraid of judgment and rejection, barely made eye contact, lacked presence, had low emotional intelligence, was scared of vulnerability and didn't know how to really connect. Some friends occasionally commented that I always "seemed so busy", I was never available to just hang out and connect. Underneath the self-created constant busyness, truthfully I didn't know how to feel real connection with others.

What area of life do you avoid because it scares you or you don't know how to do it?

Once in a one-on-one conversation with a female friend, as my eyes darted to and fro unaware of my body while talking really fast, she lovingly guided my face into direct eye contact. It was as if I had settled into a form-fitting space suit for the first time. My mind got quiet and time seemed to slow down as I could feel my whole body, two feet standing on the ground. I could hear my breathing and best of all, through a soft warm openness in the center of my chest, I felt connected to her. It was as if, for the first time, I could actually feel what a real alive human connection felt like. It was so incredibly beautiful and something part of me had been searching for my whole life; I just hadn't known how.

Just because she had gifted me with a brief glimpse of possibility, that didn't mean it was wired into my nervous system as an actualized everyday stable baseline. But I kept practicing being embodied, open and more present in each future conversation.

With humility and undefended self-honesty about the recurring feedback of my lack of presence and emotional openness, I proceeded with a genuine willingness to learn something new. I read books, went to various workshops, learned *Authentic Relating* and *Getting Real* and did attachment healing work. I practiced, played and experimented a lot with being real, open, transparent, emotionally vulnerable, listening, and feeling connection in relationship, friendship, community, family and strangers.

My favorite relational practice by far was the Argentinian Tango. It helped me deepen my ability to be embodied, initiate and lead, while also being attuned and connected to my partner. I also learned to generate masculine and feminine sexual polarity, while flowing together to the rhythm and embellishing creative moves within the Tango form. And it was so fun and sexy!

How do you practice loving more deeply and feeling more connected while staying in your own embodied center?

Alongside all of this personal development over the past decade, there had been a parallel track of career, purpose and professional development to be of service to others. Thousands of hours of reading, daily meditation and integral life practices, watching videos and listening to audio lectures and podcasts, and attending more workshops and experiential trainings than I can recall. I earned a Master's Degree in Psychology and a two-year program with the developmental masters, Integral Coaching Canada® (ICC). In practice, since 2010, I have done more than 10,000 hours coaching individual and couples clients, hundreds of hours speaking and facilitating groups, and dozens of retreats.

After all of this active driving development, the next phase of the journey would involve deeper relaxation, stillness and Awakening. Amidst a sufficient but light work schedule, the next couple years of my life involved much more solitude. Hundreds of hours of meditation and being still enabled a profound internal transformation. Many inner states came and went during this unlearning and disintegration phase; some involved the relaxing of fixed identities and mental constructs as the mind went quiet and the personal self began fading in and out.

For some people this process can be terrifying or feel like a death of sorts as masks fall away and past unresolved trauma comes up. For others who have done significant somatic healing of trauma and who understand what the Awakening process involves, it can be a blissful deepening and ecstatic expansion. As the energetic pathways open and fixated attention is liberated from identifications with mind and sense of self, infinite Openness, deep Presence and Non-Dual Loving Awareness remains.

Although for some, personal development often begins in order to get out of pain, overcome struggle or develop healthy connection with others (all of which were initial drivers for me), ultimately our development, self-actualization and self-transcendence are not just for our own personal gain. The more our hearts open and Awareness expands, the more of the world we are able to feel, be aware of, and Open as, while ultimately feeling the interconnectedness of how we are all in this together.

Life continues on, though eventually not as much as a destination, but a continuously evolving process amidst an infinite changeless perfection. Some feel it all as Love, others as Presence, or together as loving Presence. It has been called many names over the millennia, although all our human minds can really do is point to the intimate felt sense of the Unspeakable.

Ultimately our healing, development and Awakening is not just for our own ego, but so that we may be increasingly used as liberated and loving instruments of service. As transmitters of greater potential it includes the full, dynamic range of our humanity from our humility, unconsciousness and continuous learning to our ninja skillfulness, glorious greatness, and the all-embracing beauty of Loving Presence Itself.

This is a glimpse into my transformation and rising.

What has yours been like?

www.ingramcontent.com/pod-product-compliance
Lightning Source LLC
Chambersburg PA
CBHW040801150426
42811CB00056B/1114